LIFE IN THE POND,
Still Dreaming of the
PUDDLE

More Reflections of My Life's Journey
in the Bahamas and America

BERTRAM SMITH

Life in the Pond, Still Dreaming of the Puddle: More Reflections of My Life's Journey in the Bahamas and America
Copyright © 2024 Bertram Smith

All rights reserved.

No part of this book may be reproduced, stored, or transmitted by any means—whether auditory, graphic, mechanical, or electronic—without written permission of both publisher and author, except in the case of brief excerpts used in critical articles and reviews. Unauthorized reproduction of any part of this work is illegal and is punishable by law.

Published by Impel Books
https://www.bookstoinspireus.com/

Cover and Interior Design by Jose Pepito
Inspire Books

Print ISBN: 979-8-9911908-2-4
Ebook ISBN: 979-8-9911908-3-1

Printed in the United States

Contents

Dedication vii
Foreword ix
Introduction xi

Always Becoming 1
In the Pond 5
Land of Opportunity 7
I Guess I Am One of the Lucky Ones 10
A Love-Hate Relationship 16
The Conversation Yet to Be Had 22
And They Will Need Your Wisdom 25
Open the Door 29
A Burrito Never Tasted So Good 33
The Edge of Eleven 38
Never Too Busy 41
Living with Regrets 42
Speaking about Regrets in Life 45
See You in the Mornin' 51
You Can Become Drunk on Too Much TV 52
A Prisoner of Words 54
Joy 57
When We Come Together 61
Sometimes 64

Of the Many Things You Have Taught Me	67
Throwback	73
Talking to My Good Friend Jose the Other Day	74
They Don't Live Like That Anymore	77
The One Thing You Need to Know About the Pond	79
Guacamole	81
My Wife Says No	83
It never fails to amaze me	85
I Wanted to Care for You	87
She Was This Girl I Wanted to Know	89
Death Up Close	93
Life in the Pond, Still Dreaming of the Puddle	98
The Day Cracker Brought—Of All Things—A Fish to School	103
My Dad, the Theologian	108
My Dad Was a Philosopher Too	112
I Used to Hear My Dad Say	114
Milton	116
Alton and the Dog	120
I Love You, Matilda—Picky-Head and All	123
Love Never Dies	127
After the Storm	130
You Saved Me (An Ode)	132
My First Introduction to My Own Blackness	135
I Ain't No African	141
Speaking of Africa	145
My Mom and All Her Sisters	150
Like Shifting Sand	153
Conflicted and Torn	156

They All Look at Me and Wonder	158
In the Pond	159
Thank God for Ronald Reagan	161
We Used to Take It All for Granted	163
About the Author	167
About the Illustrator	168

Dedication

I dedicate this book to the three main loves of my life in this life—my beautiful and darling wife, Leslie, and my pride and joy, my two daughters, Falashade and Jamani.

My wife is truly one of the greatest inspirations to me. She is my partner in life, my chief critic, and my greatest encourager. She is the bedrock of our family, the one who exudes love in whichever form that may take.

My two daughters, as I have said many times, are simply two of the most beautiful young people that I know. They have played an invaluable role in shaping and molding me into the father and human being that I am today. With no fear of reprimand or gentle hurt to feelings—or ego—they help to keep me grounded and walking lowly and with integrity.

I love all three of them immensely, perhaps more than they will ever know. This book is dedicated to them precisely because they have enjoyed/endured this amazing journey with me.

Foreword

A very popular and powerful adage is "You can take the man out of the country, but you cannot take the country out of the man." After reading the author's first book, *From the Puddle to the Pond*, and attempting to read his second book, *Life in the Pond, Still Dreaming of the Puddle*, I am sure the reader will agree with the above adage as it applies to the author, Bertram 'Bert' Smith.

It is quite easy for the reader to conclude that despite the author living in the proverbial 'Pond' (America), he continues to dream of the proverbial 'Puddle' (Andros and the Bahamas).

I invite the reader to follow the developmental stages in the author's life as he traverses his miraculous journey from childhood to manhood by reading his poems from the beginning to the end.

It is also hoped that you, the reader, will ascertain from the author's writing that he hails from a home with parents of deep spiritual conviction who instilled in him a genuine love for God, family, and humanity.

Lucy Smith Taylor
Associated Pastor, Evangelistic Pentecostal Church, Inc.
Nassau, Bahamas
Retired Educator, Ministry of Education
Nassau, Bahamas

Introduction

In my first book, *From the Puddle to the Pond*, I wanted to share adventurous stories, lessons learned, and insights from my journey from my native Bahamas to America. The condition—we might say plight—of the immigrant is that no matter how long we live in a foreign land, we cannot rid ourselves of the memories of home.

So, almost naturally, the thought came to mind to write a follow-up to *From the Puddle*. And since, as I have already intimated, it is difficult to let go of the land of one's birth, I decided to call this second offering—as you might have guessed—*Life in The Pond, Still Dreaming of the Puddle*.

In this book, as with virtually all of my writings, I try to engage the reader and challenge us to make our own sense out of the rule-bending style. In this attempt, I want to challenge you even further: I want you to have some fun with this one. I want to see if you can discern which home—the Puddle or the Pond—I prefer more. Of course, to everyone who asks, my answer is always the same. I, like many emigrants to America, see myself as belonging to two countries and having two homes. I root for both of them, and I am critical of aspects of both.

However, I challenge you for the simple reason that I am not quite sure just how honest I am with that oft refrain. I am also reminded of Jesus' words, "You cannot serve two masters," (countries, in this case) because, as Jesus said, if you try, you will hate one and love the other; you will be devoted to one and despise the other (Matthew 6:24). Well, therein lies the rub, as William Shakespeare once said.

Of course, Jesus is right! Therefore, I will leave it up to you, my illustrious reader and partner in this transaction, to make the determination.

Always Becoming

With all of her flaws
I still love her
In her
You can breathe
Dream
Become
Or
Just be
The salt-and-pepper-haired man riding on his motorbike
Down the highway
Open to the world
Straddling the big ole wide lane
Can't tell him he is not free
It's funny how she is always changing
Reinventing
Always becoming
Confident
Some say she's much too cocky and too sure of herself
Yet I love her
She sees herself as a leader

Even while she is uncomfortable with being what she was meant to be
There is so much beauty in her
Her people
In the cities
And out in the hinterlands
Ruled by basic common sense
And uncommon collective decency
A faith in God
And country
Live in her long enough
Travel within her
North to South
East to West
Her stunning and breathtaking coastlines
Her equally vast mesmerizing rolling jagged high flat and undulating interior
You cannot help but mutter how God has blessed her
A magnificent blend of peoples and different cultures
No wonder she is the envy of all the other nations
She is not perfect
Far from it
And that's because she is always becoming

In the Pond

In the Pond
There is always a dream being held out to you
Dangling in front of you
Sometimes it comes in the form of a lottery ticket
Or Jeopardy
You think you can just reach out and grab it
As a few have
The few you can say that were lucky
But this does not stop the others from trying
Dreaming
People ask me
Why do you love the Pond
Why do you love it so much
And all that I can say is
In the Pond
Unlike in the Puddle where life can sometimes feel suffocating
At least you can breathe
And every day
Wake up to a new dream

Land of Opportunity

When I first came to this country
The Pond
Struggling right from the start
Like so many others
I came with next to nothing
Many times I did not know where that next meal would be coming from
But with drive
Determination
A healthy dose of naivete
And a halfway decent attitude
In the Pond
This land of opportunity
You can rise to heights unimagined
See me
A young man
Peddling on an old rusted and screechy bicycle that we had bought at a yard sale
Only ten dollars the precocious young entrepreneur had said
As his proud mom smiled

Beamed at his already budding entrepreneurial skills
I pulled up to the man behind the restaurant
I didn't know it then
But he was the general manager
The one in charge
Always polite and respectful
Life in the Puddle had taught me well
I said
Excuse me sir
I am looking for work
And
Do you have anything that I can do
He said
No
Sorry young man
Don't have anything at the moment
But here is something I have learned
Even in the Pond
Especially in a place like the Pond
Your attitude will always make room for you
Get you into the tightest of places
That man he paused
Reconsidered
Right there on the spot
He just made a way out of nowhere for me
He said
Hold up young man
Are you a student at the university
Yes sir I said

Well I guess you really need a job eh
Sure do sir
I said really piling it on
I guess he could see the look of desperation in my eyes
He said
I tell you what we'll do
You come back tomorrow
We'll have you take out the trash
Wash and scrub down all the cans
And when all of the workers are gone
You can hose and scrub the floors
I thanked him profusely
This was my first job in the Pond
My ticket to the future
I just knew it
I cannot begin to tell you how elated I was
I wobbled away on my old screechy rusted bike
Thinking to myself
The Pond
No wonder they call it the land of opportunity

I Guess I Am One of the Lucky Ones

Sometimes
When I get to thinking
I can't help but wonder
Who am I
What am I
And how did I get here
Really
Am I lucky
Blessed
Or
Am I just a coward
A deserter
As some would say
Lacking in backbone and tenacity
Why exactly did I leave the Puddle
It's always an open question
One that I have asked myself time and time again
A man once said to me

Standing on the dock at Potters Cay
He said
Whatever you do
You can't leave
You mustn't leave he said
You have to stay
You have to stand up and fight
Go off he said
Get the best education you can get
But you must come back and help to build your country
This is your country he said with emphasis
He said that there were too many of us who didn't have the backbone
He said that if you are not prepared to fight
Fight for your country
The land of your birth
Then you have vacated your rights to a country
He was passionate
And said it with emphasis
And you certainly don't have the right to criticize
The right to criticize anything that goes on in that country
But the sun was already setting on the idea
And furthermore
All that patriotic oratory he was spewing
He was all drunk and wobbling when he said it
So I left
Left the Puddle
There are more like me
Divided

Torn and conflicted
Some who would jump at the opportunity to be given wings
Any sort of wings
Wings so that they too can fly away
Fly far
Far away from places like the Puddle
Even though there is so much beauty in the Puddle
In the Puddle it is so easy to reflect
And there are so many things that are a reflection of you
You can find peace and tranquility in the Puddle
Even if the Puddle is sometimes stifling
And suffocating
And you feel like you are living your life in a bubble
Life in the Pond is not easy either
There is a different kind of struggle
I call it headwind
Some would argue it's far worse
At least in the Puddle you are not constantly being defined
Labeled
Told who you are what you can and cannot do
My friends and relatives back there
In the Puddle
They simply don't understand
They think that life in the Pond is all that it is cracked up to be
All rosy
They watch it all the time they say in the movies and on TV
So
There I was
Once again talking to a good friend of mine

She was sitting on the stoop in the backyard
I was standing leaning on the door post
The paint all cracked and peeling
We had known each other for quite some time
We had gone to school together
I was back home
Just for a visit
We talked
Talked for a while
Reminisced
She said I was lucky
And
That I didn't know how lucky I was
She said she would do anything to get away from this godforsaken place
And she reminded me again of how lucky I was
I don't know
All I know is that I am in love with the Puddle
It is home
A place that I can call my own
A place to always come back to
Then
As if to corner me
Pin me down
She said
See
That is the whole point
That is exactly the point I am making
You don't live here

And as if to really shove the knife in and wrench it
Make it hurt
She goes
Who are you
What are you
Really
You are not from here anymore
You get to come just for a visit
Be a tourist
And then leave
She said
There are many of us who do not have that choice
And will never have the opportunity to even consider leaving
We are stuck she said in this sometimes-maddening place
Few jobs
Limited chances
Opportunities
And it's never safe around here she says
Casting her wary eyes around
Crime is on the rise
And who do I know downtown even if there was a job opening
She wonders out loud
At least you get to go and live over there
In the land of opportunity
And the free
We talked
She and I
Late into the night
And as I drove away

Pensively
I couldn't help but think
That maybe she was right
I guess I am one of the lucky ones

A Love-Hate Relationship

We all have it and feel it
It is a feeling that those of us who had to leave know all too well
Watch us
Every last one of us
We have this strange attachment
Estrangement
Deeply emotional
And psychological
Call it a love-hate relationship
This I love em today but I can't stand em tomorrow type of attitude with where we come from
It all depends on the day
The news
And what's happening at the time
We love certain things about our little puddles of course
For example
We all love and cherish the memories
Ah the memories
Some pleasant
Some not so pleasant

The memories that won't fade
Can't die
And there are many
We still want to hold on to them
Cling to them
No matter how we try
We just can't seem to let go of the memories
Here in the Pond
Away from the Puddle
They help to sustain us
Fortify us
Against the sometimes daunting headwinds that come against us in the Pond
The memories
We talk about them to the point of ad nauseum
Nostalgically
At parties
At gatherings
And every time we meet
Come together
Watch us
Every last one of us
We still eat our familiar foods
Peas and rice
Crack conch
Fry fish
Steam and stew fish too
You can't leave out the boil fish and Johnny cake
Crawfish

Macaroni and cheese
Lots and lots of potato salad
And a side of wet coleslaw
We dig up the same old familiar tunes
Tunes to wind and grind to
Calypso
Merengue
Soca
Junkanoo
Some Bob Marley to match the militant mood we are feeling
A mood of strange defiance and anger
We don't even know why
Then watch us
Every last one of us
Drown the hate part
That part of us that has turned into commiserate misery
Drown it in whatever flows or is flowing
That is comforting
Numbing
It could be Bacardi
Campari
Rum punch
Two and three bottles of Heineken
Or whatever else is still left
And gouge ourselves on the many memories
What do we love about the places we come from
The people of course
They add to all the sweet memories
Though we sometimes speak ill of them

The ones we know
And the ones we don't even know
They are our people still
Part of us
They always epitomize for us the Puddle
We see ourselves in their many faces
In their triumphs
Their accomplishments
And achievements
Especially on the world stage
They fill us up with an endless sense of pride
And joy
Something to cheer and brag about to our couple of friends in the Pond
Did you see the Olympics today
That girl Shaunae
Now that's my girl
Shaunae
The one who doesn't just run
But who glides like an eagle and makes us all proud
Proud to be Bahamian
What we don't like about our little puddles
Wherever they may be
Are the very same things that forced us to leave in the first place
The new way of life
The one that has painted over the life we once knew
Admired
Choked it

Snuffed it out
The lack of real chances
The unfairness built into the implacable wall
And layered
Brick by brick
That has become ever so formidable and impenetrable
It confronts you every time you go downtown
It's the frustration
The frustration that confronts you at almost every turn
The implacable who you know over what you know
That common and irritating refrain
Borne in the questions
The questions that are meant to define
Quantify
And qualify you
Like
Who your people
Your last name
Which island
It creates this mild and somber consternation
A nagging irritation inside of you
And fuels the anger
Every time you hear it
Experience it
It creates this feeling of just not being able to spread one's wings
To their fullest extent
And just fly
Soar

The way you and God wanted it to be
To just be able to fly
Soar like Shaunae
To be and become all you want to be
Unhindered
Uninhibited
In the land of one's birth

The Conversation Yet to Be Had

The problem with the Pond
Its greatest challenge
Drawback
Perhaps its greatest impediment to its own success
And getting worse
Is the issue of race
That age-old question
When you come from somewhere else
Outside of the Pond
You just feel like screaming
Like Maniac McGee
Talk
Talk
Talk will you
Why don't you just talk to each other
In the Pond
We somehow just don't like to talk about it
I don't know what it is

Or why
Have we become too comfortable with it
An uneasy status quo
Or
Is it too painful
Or have we convinced ourselves that to not talk about it means that it
As a problem
And all the other problems surrounding it
Do not exist
Maybe it's because we don't like to look upon sin
Our own sins
And then I am reminded of Nathaniel Hawthorne
Yes
The race question
That thorny issue in the side of the Pond
That stain
That headwind that I am convinced is holding her back
Keeping her from running
Chasing after
And achieving
And fulfilling
Her God-given potential
We just refuse to talk about it
The problem
Let it come out in the open
A forbidden topic
Taboo

Even though it's never far from the surface in all matters and in every quarter
Ever present
Oh yes
We may joke about it
Make light of it
Skip around it
It all tells of
And reflects
Our discomfort and uneasiness when it comes to this question
But never broaching it
Confronting it head on
No
We don't want to talk about it
Certainly not sitting around the round and wide red table
Yet it is the conundrum of every room
The real X factor
Here
In the Pond
You can say that it is the conversation still waiting to be had

And They Will Need Your Wisdom

You have to stop and wonder sometimes
Why was I dragged from the pit of my existence
Forcefully
Brutally
And collectively
It doesn't matter whether you are from the Pond or one of the puddles
Sold
Dragged through the hot sandy desert
Shackled
Across the just-as-treacherous wide sea
Again
Shackled
Bought
Beaten
Lied on
And mistreated
Why

And then that little voice whispers like the breeze
It whispers
Maybe
Just maybe
It was to fulfill a purpose
Destiny
Maybe it was to save lives
The easy gentle voice
It says
And I always knew
They would need your wisdom

Open the Door

Open the door
Open it
I promise you
Just a crack
A sliver
Dare to open it I say
And watch me walk right through
As if the door had always been open there to me
For me
Watch me step right through
And in
And take command of the room
Take my place
My rightful place
Because
If there is one thing I know
No
Not one
Two
Even three

You have Smarts and you have this thing called Attitude
With Boldness permeating the two
When it comes to taking command of a room
It's my birthright
My destiny
Who and what I was meant to be
No need to fear me
I can't help but be who and what I was born to be
I am bold
Fearless
Undaunted
It's not that I am better
It's just that Smarts Boldness and Attitude always accompany me wherever I go
Some people call it machismo
Some say charisma
I don't have a name for it
It's just me

A Burrito Never Tasted So Good

Those were the years
Middle school teacher
Building those unforgettable relationships with my students
Watching them grow
And learn
But it was the unusual things they did
The things that caught my attention
Always would catch me by surprise
Completely off guard
And make me smile when no one else was around
Like this one young man who decided to give me his burrito
His mom had made it
It was wrapped ever so tight and lovingly
It was perhaps his favorite meal
He had seen the other kids
Just before the break
The end of the school year
Stopping by my desk

And dropping off gifts
But he himself had none to give
Or so he thought
No explaining on my part could soothe or put his mind at rest
He just wanted to give
Then
In a move that caught me off guard
And completely by surprise
He said
Here
You can have my burrito
No amount of protestation and deferring on my part could dissuade
He said
No
You can have it
Really
I don't want it
What else could I say
What else could I do
I thanked Jose
Gave him a hug
And placed the burrito on my desk
Along with all the other gifts
Later on that day
After they had all filed out
Gone home
I sat there
At my desk

Read the sweet notes they had all left behind
I saved the burrito for last
Finally
And without even thinking
I began to peel back the wrappings
The foil
Then the double layer of paper
The burrito was soft and slightly damp
Still warm
A warmth that said love
A mother's love
I couldn't get over how neatly it was wrapped
Something told me to warm it up
But I couldn't wait
The sweet savory smell was already reaching tingling and exciting my nose
I sat back in my chair
Tossed my feet up
Thought about Mrs. Cordova
The love that must have gone into the making of that burrito
Then I thought about Jose
The joy
And the pains of being his teacher
How he had struggled early on
His innate smartness
The mischievous side that sometimes demanded
And commanded
My attention
I bit into that soft still-warm burrito

Stuffed with peppers and onions
Spiced with love and jalapeños
I savored it
I took another bite
Then another
Allowing the clash of the potpourri of home-cooked tastiness
and goodness to tumble around inside my mouth
Imagined the love and care that went into it
Equally
The thoughts
The memories
Of the smart
Troubled kid
How
Just moments before I had to get onto him
Yet the love
Pure and not fake
The forgiveness that is constant with kids like Jose
Yet the difficulties
The trials
And the challenges of teaching one like him too
Kids
I munched down on that burrito one more time
Thought about Jose
The innate intelligence
The mischievousness
The troubles
The challenges
The trials we had been through together

And the many burritos I had enjoyed over the years
But this one was different
It was special
It smacked of satisfaction
And I couldn't exactly put my finger on it
Why I enjoyed it so much
Whether it was the tastiness of the love that Mrs. Cordova had packed into it
Or was it just sweet revenge

The Edge of Eleven

She came
And plunked herself down right beside me
In the vacant seat by my desk
Can I tell you something she says
She has just turned eleven and has made it to sixth grade
A sister of one of my students
Not even one of mine
And I am wondering why I have to befriend and be a counselor to this errant little kid
But she cannot contain herself
Irrepressible
Oblivious
And loves to chat
She has begun to discover the sway of her powers over boys
She loves to share her joys and her woes
All related
Somehow
To the many boys who come streaming through her life like a long line of train cars
Today it is the same old story
Okay she starts

You tell me what you think I should do okay
And I brace myself
She is oblivious to the fact that I am an adult
And a teacher
Breathlessly
She goes
So there is this boy right
He likes me
I know he likes me
He gives me half of his Oreos
And some Takis
All the time
And whenever he sees me
He tells everyone he likes me right
But doesn't have the nerve to tell it to me himself
He's kind of cute
Stays in trouble
I can almost see myself liking him
Then remembering that I am still there she says
Tell me
What do you think
And I am too afraid to speak
Open my mouth
Say anything
Better to keep my mouth shut
Because I know
To a sixth grader
The bliss of today
Will more than likely come crashing down in bitter divorce by tomorrow

Never Too Busy

My youngest daughter called me the other day
She said
Dad
Are you busy
And
Can I talk to you
Little does she know
When it comes to her
A gem
One of the true jewels in my crown
I am never too busy

Living with Regrets

Sometimes
Sadly
In life
You will end up with regrets
The last time I went back
Back home to the Puddle
And the island I grew up on and still call home
I did not get a chance to see her
Not that I didn't want to
Or was not curious how things had turned out
I asked them
How she was doing
And was she well
Oh you know her they asked in that sing-song voice
That sing-song voice I had somehow lost
Yes I said quietly
She lives right over there they said
Just over that hill right there
And I looked

From the little strip of an airport I could almost see the house
to which they were pointing
But did I even want to go
Over the hill
Right there they had said
It seemed so close yet so far away
I had to ask myself
Should I go
Or no
Or did I even want to take that risk
Many years had passed between us
The thought of rekindling an old flame
Showing my now slightly-haggard face
Filled me with a vague sense of trepidation
They said
Do you want us to tell her you are here and want to see her
No
No
No I rushed
Then the excuse came
It just tripped right off of my tongue
I don't know that we have time
The plane is about to come
It won't take long they said
But again I demurred
All I could think of was all those years that had come between
And how so much must have changed
I thought about it
Reflected

Reflected on how maybe I should go
Peep in on her
Say hello
Just for old times' sake
She had such a beautiful face and smile
But my thoughts conflicted
Would not let me go
The little prop engine plane would soon come I knew
I couldn't afford to miss the flight
Was it what I believed
Or was it just a convenient excuse
An excuse to maybe hide my cowardice
And right then I knew
I knew this was one of those moments
A moment I would live to regret
Maybe for the rest of my life

Speaking about Regrets in Life

Flying is just not something I enjoy
So it is kind of strange
That one of my greatest regrets in life
Would have to do with flying
He heard me talking
I could tell he had been listening for a while
Trying to place my accent
We all do it
Sometimes it's hard to tell
Especially when you have been away for such a long time
We were standing on the lonely tarmac
Cracked with weeds sprouting right out of the pavement
Just us
And my small party
He wanted to know what I was
My identity
I said
I am a Bahamian

I thought so he responded
He was too
He was delighted to meet me
Make my acquaintance
A Bahamian he said
With joyful emphasis
You must be living abroad
Wow
I think
Destiny
How fickle
At that moment
Reunited
We look at each other and just knew we were kinfolk
Brothers
He said to me
You come on up front
Help me fly the plane
Be my copilot he said and smiled
Little one-propeller plane
Looked like a tub or dingy boat with wings
Suspicious and unreliable
A little bit scary and dangerous
Quite unworthy of the skies
That's when the true cowardice in me came tumbling out
When it comes to flying
I told him
He was a much better man than me
I couldn't do it

I couldn't even will myself to do it
No matter how hard I tried
It's okay he said
Years later
Comes the ever-nagging outstanding regret
No
It's not okay
Looking back
Why was I so afraid
Weak
Why couldn't I just stand up
Be a man
Like my newfound friend
My brother
You know how they always tell you
You have to face your fears
Face up to them
Why
Why couldn't I just do it
Why did I have to go and embarrass
Disappoint my brother
The one who just wanted so desperately to be reacquainted
Oh how I wish I could travel back in time
See me
Watch me
Up there
High above those fluffy puffy white clouds
My hands firmly and tightly gripping the half-moon of a wheel
Chatting

Engaging in all sorts of friendly banter
About life in the Pond
He had never been
And how were things still in the Puddle
And I would look over at my newfound friend
My brother
And smile
Beaming with delight
Oh how I wish I could go back there
What would I not give for just those few moments
But I know I can't
So
Yes
To this day
I say it all the time
The others I can live down
But this
Without a doubt
Is one of my greatest regrets in life

See You in the Mornin'

She said she just wanted to go to sleep
And
Leave me alone now
Can't you see I am finished with you
She said she was tired
And why couldn't I understand
Go now
Leave me alone she said
Go
Get away I said
And just when I thought it was in sheer disgust
She looked at me
Smiled
And said
I'll see you in the mornin'

You Can Become Drunk on Too Much TV

Here in the Pond
You have to be careful
You can become complacent
Lose that early drive and determination
The hunger to succeed
You can become drunk from watching too much TV
There is always something on
Sports
Entertainment
Games
Like The Dating Game
Or The Price is Right
And the endless array of comedy and talk shows
To a young person
Living in the Pond
Or coming here
The best advice I can give to you would be to resist the TV
Cradle in your arms a book instead

You can become drunk from watching too much TV
Idle time
Games
And video games
Before you know it
Life can lull you to sleep
Make you drowsy
A sluggard
Slow down your row
Just like that proverbial frog in a kettle
Cause you to lose that grit
The grittiness you had
Came with
That dogged determination and drive to succeed
That verve
Sooner
Rather than later
If you are not careful
Life in the Pond
Can turn you into a bit of a slug

A Prisoner of Words

I read in the papers the other day
Saw where your mom had passed away
And it saddened me
Made me feel guilty
Guilty for all the years that had intervened
Come between us
And the words
That made me such a prisoner
A prisoner of my words
The words
That paralyzed
And immobilized me
I remember your mom like it was yesterday
Beautiful
Just like you
That look of concern she often wore
Always a look of concern
Was it for me
Or was it for you
The news it came

Hit me hard
Left me feeling sad and not knowing what to do
Should I reach out to you
In spite of those words
Hurtful I know
Words flung
Unlike the boomerang
Can never be taken back
They often paralyze
Immobilize us
Turn us into prisoners
Prisoners of words
And then there is the slippage of time
No friend to any of us
But it is mostly the words
Abrupt
Brief
All in anger
When I saw how you were slipping away
The passage of time
The way we parted
Not on good terms
Slamming down the phone and the words
Goodbye
The final goodbye
Once and forever
Words
Those words
Sometimes

Words
Our words
Can keep us bound in chains
Locked up as if in a prison
Paralyzed
Immobilized
A helpless
Hapless prisoner

Joy

I remember when my first daughter was born
It felt so unreal
Like I was floating
Drifting sweetly in and through the air
Walking among the clouds
Climbing and climbing
And all around me was peaceful and calm
Still
Muted
The birds had stopped chirping
The cars horns had gone silent
No sound of big trucks chortling and snorting
Snarling
Everything just seemed at a standstill
A whisper like soft air
And it felt like I was the only one left in the whole wide world
Just me
Happy beyond words
Oblivious
Yes

It was just me
In a world twice removed
A world of fluttering colors like butterflies
That was when I discovered
It first hit me
Dawned on me
That you have to have something
Something concrete
Tangible
A reality
Not just a concept
Not even a thing
But a lifeform
A person
That had come to life
And that was forever attached to you
No matter how tiny
No matter how small or frail
To discover
And to know
Real joy

When We Come Together

Somewhere in a corner of the Pond
When we all come together
All expatriates who
For some reason or another
Had left
Left the Puddle
And made our way across the largest of all ponds
We would reminisce
Tell stories
Sing the same old songs from growing up in the Puddle
It doesn't matter that we are much older now
And that time had changed us—and was still changing us
We would cook our native foods
All the foods we were raised on
Foods that might be killing us but tasted too good and are too sentimental to give up
We play the same ole music and we laugh
This is our way of keeping all the memories alive
And to soothe ourselves and each other
Life in the Pond has a way of working on your nerves

So we play the same old songs and we laugh
Tell stories
Everyone walking around with a plastic cup
Or a brown paper bag
These are our comfort now
Remind us of when we were back in the Puddle
Our attempts to hold onto sanity
As if we are the displacements
Refugees of war
Imagine that
Sanity
Peace
Happiness
In a red plastic cup
Or a brown paper bag
And so we laugh and we carry on
It's our way of drowning the sadness
The way some people carry theirs
Leaning on their elbows and staring out of windows
We prefer to drown our sadness
Our plight of being stuck in life
Between not being able to go back
Or thinking that you can't
And the headwind we experience every day in the Pond
The Pond
You can really feel stuck
A job
Usually just a piece of a job

Something we would not be found dead doing if we were back in the Puddle

Enough to pay the rent we say

But yet not knowing

Not knowing which way to go

At least we can still congregate

Come together

Tell stories of days long gone by

Of life

Back in the Puddle

Sometimes

Sometimes
In the Pond
In the middle of the madness
You just have to stop
Pause
Ponder
Ask yourself
What is the meaning of life
And is this the best that life has to offer
Am I better off here
In the Pond
Or do I belong back there
In the Puddle
I am thinking all of this
As I sit hopelessly stuck in traffic
Enraged motorists honking their horns and yelling out into the open air
We are all buried in twelve lanes of traffic
All in a maddening standstill
I think about the life

The plight I am in
And I have to ask
What is the meaning of life
And is this the best that life has to offer
Am I better off here
In this Pond
Or would I be better off back there
In the Puddle
I don't know
I just don't know
I am bored
I fish haphazardly and randomly in my shirt pocket because I feel something
Out comes a lottery ticket
I stare at it
Vacuously
And the blur of a dream comes into focus
As quick as it comes
And brings a smile to my face
In the same way
It is gone

Of the Many Things You Have Taught Me

My lover
My wife
The love of my life
How was I supposed to know
That those many years ago
When I met you
Chanced you
Sitting beneath that flimsy tree
You and your two friends
That you would be the one
Chiseled out of life
By the ever-loving compassionate and gracious Craftsman
Sculptor
Creator of the universe
He had compassion on me
How could I have known
Back then
In the land of shallowness and just dreams

That we
Our love would grow up together
Like two tender
Clinging
Cleaving saplings
Stubborn elm trees
And you would become all that you have become to me
You have become my school teacher
My instructor
In oh just so many things touching life
Of all the things you have taught me
And schooled me in
The most surprising
And enduring
Touches on the topic and matter of love
I thought I had it figured out
You know how those things go
The essence and the meaning of love
That is until I met you
Not for the first time
But again
When you showed up anew
Again
When our lives
Already a battle
Got turned into another battle
Yet another battle for us to have to contend with
That's when the teaching
And the real lesson began

It was then you opened up your heart wide
Wider than I had ever seen before
Sometimes you just don't know how wide
How wide the windows of our hearts can swing open
Reminding us of the windows of Heaven
That's when you became my schoolmaster my teacher and my instructor
You taught me the true meaning and essence of the puzzle
That puzzle we call love
That's when you revealed to me
And the world
Yet another layer of you
That's why I love you
Those many layers
Surprises
The many sides of you
This last time
Who could have ever known
Imagine
The route the lessons would take
I used to think I knew the true and complete meaning of love
Until you showed up
Again
You showed up again
Just like you always do
Not that you had ever left or gone away somewhere
But you have this amazing way about you
Always showing up
New

Like the dew
And the seasons
This time
Under such difficult circumstances
The subject and the lesson
Once again
Turned to love
Of all the lessons you have taught me
Impressed upon me
That have stayed with me
That will never leave me
This one we will crown it and just say eternal
Who would have thought
After all these years
And all the lessons taught
That there would be yet one more lesson to teach
Love
You taught
Is best taught
Through actions not words
For you showed me
Love is not about such trivial things
Not words
No
Not even deeds
When that moment came
All through the battle that rocked us and tested us
Put us under such stress and duress
Like never before

You didn't express your love for me in words or deeds
What I noticed
And what impressed me beyond this life
Was simply how you came and always stayed
I noticed that you were always there
Always right there beside me
Always there for me
By my side
Whenever I would cast a weak and feeble look around
And no matter what came next
Or what the battle threw our way
No matter what time of day or night
You were always there
You would cleave
Hover
And never leave

Throwback

My wife and I
Leaving the house early one morning
Trying to beat the Atlanta traffic
Noticing the traffic is unusually light this morning my wife says
Ah look
We have the roads all to ourselves today
And I don't know why
But it made me think of growing up on the island of Andros
When you would be lucky to see one car pass by in an hour
And what an event
People working in their fields along the roadside
Or in their rocky front yards
Would all stop and go
Who da
Then they would wave with whatever they had in their hands
My mom
Working in the front yard
Between the Old House and the New House
Would smile and wave with her always-come-in-handy cutlass
Only she could make a queen's wave
With an object like this
And make it not look menacing at all

Talking to My Good Friend Jose the Other Day

And how for him the sixth time was the charm
He is not like me
Everybody's story different
He had to brave the Rio Grande
And the coyotes
To get here
Now life for him
In the Pond
Is grand
He doesn't have to eat ham and eggs sandwiches everyday no more
And he doesn't have to always be looking over his shoulders
Or listening out for the BAM BAM of ICE
Knocking down and tearing down the door each time they would come
Quickly
And unannounced
Terrorizing him

His pregnant wife
And five little kids
He to this day thanks God for his wife
The same way I do for mine
She is brave
And strong
Every time he would be gone
She would have to fend and provide for their family
Jose says he still doesn't know how she did it
My friend Jose and I
We have a lot in common
We like to talk
Laugh
Swap stories about our families
We both came from respective puddles
In search of a better life here in the Pond
We both know how much of a struggle life in the Pond can be
The headwind experienced every day
That is far too common
We both have big dreams
My friend Jose has his own landscaping company now
I am a teacher and a part-time instructor at a college
Our dream is to one day go back home
Our real homes
This is not it
The Pond can never take the place of home
Plant something
Help those we left behind
But today

And tomorrow
And next week
It is still just a vacuous dream
As for next year
We don't talk about that
As for that we'll just wait
Life in the Pond can sometimes be complicated

They Don't Live Like That Anymore

It's always fun when family comes to visit
They are impressed with the Pond
What's on TV
And the two cars in the garage that my wife and I still struggling to pay off
We sit around
Eat
Drink
And talk
Reminisce
We talk about the good ole days
How life growing up in the islands reflected such a sense of community
The love
Everybody loving and caring for one another
Food cooking in the kitchen that was always separate from the house
Or on three big rocks in the backyard

And then someone
Invariably
Breaks the mood
Oh
They would say
They don't live like that anymore

The One Thing You Need to Know About the Pond

When you come
If you come
And
If you decide to stay
The one thing you need to know about the Pond
Is that nothing in the Pond is real
It's all murky
Make-believe
And the brilliance of it
The genius of it
Going all the way back I suppose
To Greece
And then Rome
Is that nothing is quite what it seems
It's all such a beautiful and orchestrated mirage
Shiny
Robust and shimmery
Bursting with energy and the gleam of abundance
You would think that lack and poverty had been slain

Or at least
Banished long ago from the land
There is democracy
The longer you stay you see how that goes
Freedom
This in part is true
Though like so many things in the Pond
Grossly misunderstood
Choices
Opportunities
Deals
Steals
The hallmarks of competition
Like my young and somewhat gullible daughter and I
Skipping through the mammoth opulent grocery store
She is happy to be spending time with dad
She says
Gee Dad look at that
We are in the ice cream aisle
Wasting time because of the vast variety from which to choose
And she is excited
Because she has just spotted two tubs for only ten dollars
Two Dad
And they are only ten dollars
I am no economist or anything like that
Not much of a teacher
Or mathematician
But I found myself saying to my daughter
Honey
We should have bought them last week
When they were four-ninety-nine each

Guacamole

Our eyes met
She smiled at me
I tried to get my face to work so that I could reciprocate
She said
You want to try some
She was serving up samples of a special kind of guacamole
Seated behind a small table draped in the Mexican flag
Down one of the central aisles
I said sure
I do
And I have to compliment her on her guacamole
We got to talking
She says most people don't know how to make it
Gringos are the worst
And we both laugh
Because it is so true
I had long sworn off the stuff in the grocery stores
Pretty package
Nice label
And that's it
That's when my wife and my two daughters sauntered over

True to form
After I have broken the ice
And they had surmised that it was safe
There is enough fun
Smiles
And laughter to go around
And we all get into it
With this obvious La Matrona of the guacamole
Too much things they put in it she says with her strong
Self-confident accent
Then she gives us the run-down
The low-down
The 4-1-1
The dirt
On how to make the best guacamole
A little bit of salt and pepper
Jalapeños
Tomatoes
Cilantro
Slight squeeze of lemon or lime
That's it
That's all she says
And smiles
She has connected with us
And we are her captivated and adoring pupils
She respects the fact that we respect her
And the love we feel right there and then
The identification with one another
Hard to explain
Can only be felt by people like us
Living in the Pond

My Wife Says No

My wife says no
The ladies behind the counter they counter with yes
And
It's okay
Let the man enjoy life a little
And
It's not too much
He doesn't need it my wife rejoined
Look at him
And they all laugh
My wife is the best at deprecating humor
Especially when it comes to me
I am slightly embarrassed that I am the center of all of this attention
We are in the delicatessen line
Down at the world-famous farmers market now
And the friendly ladies
Once you get to know them
Behind this massively long counter
From all over the world

India
Sudan
Ethiopia
Pakistan
Eritrea
Have taken a liking to me
And they want to coax me into another slice of their many delights
They take pride in the work they do
Their wide array of cakes
Pies
Stuffed-with-fruits croissants
Muffins
Colorful fruit tarts
And much much more
Blushing
I say thank you
Through the corner of my eye
I see my wife coming again
And I don't want to stick around
To see who will win this fight

It Never Fails to Amaze Me

The level of self-absorption
Alienation
And obliviousness
That characterizes life in the Pond
Nobody has time
Nor do they care for each other
Not like in the Puddle
People die
Get shot
Suffer heart attacks and die
In their one-bedroom apartments
And nobody finds out
Until two weeks later
Then the family comes
They don't touch
Or care about the body sprawled out on the floor
They start rummaging high and low
For the insurance papers
They haven't seen the poor deceased for oh umpteen years
But now

In death
They love him
He was always our most favorite brother they tell the police
When the cops leave
They go back to searching
High and low
For the insurance papers
The Pond
It is the land of opportunity and dreams
And the opportunities
And the dreams
Can sometimes come high or low

I Wanted to Care for You

I wanted so badly to care for you

Love you

Anticipate your each and every need

Desire

I first saw you

Sitting there with the others

The others that didn't mean a thing to me

With eyes for you only

I called to you

We ran away

Just the two of us

Then came the embrace

I made you my own

Wanting

Ever so wanting

To be able to anticipate your each and every need

Desire

I promised you that I would always be there

Never leave

Never allow even a solitary tear that fell to your cheek to linger

Yes

Made it my lifelong goal to be a provider

A giver

A lover

And to go before you

Anticipating your each and every need

Desire

Yes

It was you I wanted

Yes

Only you

I wanted so badly to care for you

She Was This Girl I Wanted to Know

She was the first girl I met when I first came to the Pond
Mixed up
Confused
Yet tender and loving
Caring
In her own unique way
She calls me up
Asks me what I am doing
And did I want to go and see Alex Haley
The connection between us
It was there
And it wasn't
Maybe too much of our own individual plantations between us
Yes
The mental and psychological slavery that can linger
That lingers
That makes us feel like we come from two different planets
That we are different peoples

We got into a little spat
She asked if we could study together
Yes I said
I wanted to help
I liked Jan
At that point in my life
At that specific time
She was the girl I wanted to know
In a brief moment of anger
Misunderstanding
She said I was everything that she had heard about Caribbean men
Bossy
Controlling
Think they are the fathers of all the girls they meet
It was disappointing
Sad
That wall erected between us
The stereotypes
The slight hostility that lingers
Later
Jan dropped out of college
Went back to her little backwater town in Alabama
I have sometimes wondered what became of Jan
How her life turned out
I liked Jan
In those early days
Flung together in an introduction to philosophy class
Tossed together in a sea of whiteness

Just the two of us
I wanted to get to know my Black Sister
As a human being
A friend
She was from the Pond
I was from the Puddle
I felt like we had so much in common
So much we could share
So much to give
Imbue
Impart to each other
Yes
I liked Jan
Interesting
Intriguing
Briefly
Far too briefly
She was that girl I wanted to know

Death Up Close

I had never seen anyone dying before
Slow like that
Slowly
And trying to cope
So it shocked me even as I struggled to be brave
She wanted to find someone she could talk to
To confide in
So she chose me
Why not
She was calm
Rational about it
Well
As rational as one can be
Even though
On the inside
You could tell she was a ball of rage
Anger
She wanted to kill him she said
Especially at first
When she was first hit with the news

Found out
What for I asked
Why
And then I thought about it
My dumb questions
For what he put me through she said
Her voice slow
And muffled
For what he put both of us through
The hell
And the pain
The recklessness
The height of irresponsibility
The lies
All of the lies and deceptions
Some nerve he had she said
Even to stoop so low as to say I was the one who had it
And gave it to him
In this world
She said
Amidst all the attempts to be true
Truthful
Trusting
You can really get suckered
Taken in
Taken for a ride
Abused
Mistreated
Believing all the lies

And I had the nerve to love him she said
Give him the best years of my life
Now it is me
Us
Who have to suffer with this plague
This virus
That slowly
And eventually will kill me
Her four-year-old sat nearby absorbed in his paper and few pieces of crayons
His son I asked
Yes
She said
Wiping back the tears
The only good part of him that he imparted to me
That remains she says
The true joy of my life
And she cracks a smile as hard as it is
And as uncomfortable
A smile that is enigmatic
I say to myself
How strong
Even as that one solitary tear slides down her cheek
And she swipes at it
I try desperately to understand
How difficult and slow it is to feel pain vicariously
Especially when the wounded
When the dying is staring you right in the face and up close
What can you say to one

One as beautiful and still as lovely as she
Who knows all too well her own limitations
The fleeting nature of time
That's beautiful she says to the son who comes over
Intervenes
Who has created
To him
A masterpiece
With his paper
And just a few pieces of crayons
The tears fall
For the son she has to lie to
Even as she on the inside lay dying
The son
Who may grow up
And never really understand
She says she is still debating
Having that argument with herself
Whether or not to tell him
And how much
She says some days are good
Some not so good
And how she doesn't feel half the time like getting out of bed
She says she is not bitter
Or at least tries not to be
What kills her though she says
When she does allows herself to stop and think about it
Are the deaths of all her dreams
Dreams she once had

Dreams like a swarm of colorful happy fluttering dancing butterflies in the sunlight
The worst part of it she says
Is thinking
And thinking about the deaths of all those dreams
And I don't know what to say
What to do
Should I put my hand on her shoulder
Hug her
How could I
I had never seen death so up close before

Life in the Pond, Still Dreaming of the Puddle

Everyone I know
Who hails from the Puddle
Or someplace like it
And who are forced to live their lives somewhere in this Pond
Still dream about life in the puddles
We may say we don't miss it
But deep down we do
And we
Every last one of us
We wish that things could be different
If only things woulda coulda shoulda
Just been different
There is so much to love about the Puddle
Things to loathe as well
We all know what they are
And we talk about them whenever and wherever we meet
Come together
As if rehearsed

And we're reading each other's minds
We all share the guilt
Of having to leave the puddles behind
Bringing our luggage
The goods we have and can share with the world
Goods and services we wish we could impart to our own
We hold out hope
And we pray for things to change
Get better
So we could return
Go back
Build
Plant
Or do whatever
Life in the Pond is no joke
And it keeps getting worse
More and more confusing
To say the least
Especially if you are one of those
Like me
Trying to get in
At least
If you are here
One of the lucky ones
You still have a dream
It might be flung against or into the headwind
And even when we dream
It is remarkable how those dreams turn to home
How we still wear our pride in our homelands on our sleeves

Staunchly fighting for
And defending
The dreams
How they always take us back
Back across the water
The Rio Grande
To that life we once knew back in our respective puddles

The Day Cracker Brought—Of All Things—A Fish to School

A few of us kids
Growing up in the Puddle
Just didn't have much adult supervision
Which could
And sometimes did
Lead to some troubling situations
Like the time Cracker brought the fish he had caught to school
Well
Except that he didn't really bring it
It sort of just came along with him
And nobody probably would have known about it
Or cared that much
Except that
On this particular morning
The day Cracker brought the fish to school
Comatose style
It was hot

It was hot even though it was still early in the morning
And the sun had not yet peeked its head above the cedar trees
It was hot the way it was hot most of the time in Andros
And it was calm
Real calm
Not a single breeze was stirring
The perfect combination of weather and atmospheric conditions
For any scent to just rise
Swirl
And travel
Especially when you were all cramped up
Like we were
In an already miserable classroom
We were all sitting in English class
Composition writing time
Trying to focus
When someone went
Sniff
Sniff
And
Do you smell that
Someone else said
Yeah
I smell something
That's when someone else next door volunteered
Yeah I smell it too
And it smells like some kind of dead rat
There was a general and audible snicker at this last statement
And now the classroom had become a bit of a stir

Everyone kept turning around
And from side to side
And wanting to know what was that awful smell
The one that was swirling around
Easy
Easy
Calm down
Everybody just calm down the teacher said
The teacher
An always irritable middle-age light-skinned man from Jamaica
Annoyed that the class's concentration had been broken at such a critical time
Couldn't help himself and started to sniff too
He proceeded to go down each row
Poking out his nose often
All the time trying not to sniff too loudly
Not wanting to
He elicited even more snickers
Eventually the scent led straight to Cracker
Actually
To Cracker's pants pocket
Stand up you wretched little boy the teacher said
Except he said lickle
That was when the snickering and half-suppressed laughter exploded
Cracker was known for not being one of the most brightest kids in the class
And often not very attuned to things in general
But

Back there in the Puddle
We had never heard of special ed
Or differentiation
Modifications
Or anything like that
Cracker got up
Slowly
That was when we all saw it
The bulge in Cracker's front pocket
And the unmistakable double tail fin of a fish
A broad silver shad
That was sticking precariously out
The class erupted
Just fell apart
The teacher tried
But no matter how hard he tried
He could not regain control and composure in the classroom
In our little world
When that happened
And the dead fish was revealed
That was it for the day
The teacher may as well have said alright everybody pack em up and go home
Here is what we learned
Gleaned from bits and pieces of the story
Apparently
Nobody at Cracker's house had bothered to check the boy's pants pocket
Much less washed his clothes

We came to learn
That the dead fish sticking out of Cracker's pocket
Had been there for quite some time
Some surmised
And by the stench that had filled the classroom that day
We all agreed
That that fish
Sticking precariously out of Cracker's front pocket
It must have been dead
For some four days
At least

My Dad, the Theologian

Talking about the Puddle always gets me to thinking about my dad
Some of the things he would say
My dad was a wise man
And a great theologian
In a strange sort of way
His way
He never said so
And nobody ever crowned him as such
He just was
Like the time the church leader
High-ranking official
Came all the way from Nassau to put out a fire
The fire had flared up in the church
So the big-time official had to come
And he stopped by our house
My dad and my mom were sitting on the front porch relaxing
And trying to escape the summer heat
The minister wanted someone to talk to
Someone he knew

Was comfortable with
Someone he could confide in
And relate to
Someone that he maybe could get to see the enormity of the problem he was shouldering
He thought my dad
A man of the cloth too
Would be the perfect confidante
A spiritual matter had arisen
A man
Not just any man
But the pastor of one of the local churches
Had wobbled and stumbled
Badly
Though married
The pastor had slept with a woman other than his wife
A Sister in the church
So the leader came and leaned sadly on the porch rail
He sighed deeply
Several times
And throughout his side of the story
He was a perfect picture of quiet and deep distraught
Deep and thick like the heat that day
But at the same time he was hopeful
He still had my dad's shoulder to lean on
He still saw in my dad a trusted friend and coworker on the battlefield
That warm afternoon he poured out his heart
Emptied it right there in front of my dad

After his heart was empty
For he had wrung it dry
And following a lengthy silence
And more sighs
A lengthy silence between the two of them
In that moment
At that sacred hour
It looked like a meeting between the apostles Paul and Peter
Finally
The leader said
Yes my Brother
The devil is sure nuff busy
To which my dad paused
Gathered his most reasoned theological wisdom
And then responded
Yes my Brother
However
It would seem to me
That in this particular case
The devil was in the man's pants
My mom
Who was sitting there
And overheard the whole conversation
Much like Sarah in the Bible
My mom burst out laughing
The church official
Surprised
And taken aback by what my dad
The lowly theologian

Had said
And thinking that he had not heard straight
Had to ask again
What's that you say Brother
My dad said it again
One thing about my dad he was not bashful
Had no qualms about giving his firmly held well-reasoned seasoned opinions
Yes sir
My dad calmly repeated
It seems to me
That
In this particular case
Like I say
The devil was in the man's pants

My Dad Was a Philosopher Too

My dad was a businessman
Every month he went to Nassau to hawk his wares
Everyone in the settlement trusted my dad
He would sell their produce too
And bring back every penny
Even though my dad could hardly read and write
Coconuts
Limes
Guineps
Soursops
Sugar apples
Plums
Hog and scallop plums
Mangoes
Crabs
White crabs and black ones
Or whatever they would send
Oh yes

And my dad also sold his world-famous bush medicine
Well
He was known all over the Puddle for his strange strong brew
My dad was a reasonable man
A deep philosophical thinker
Like one time
A businesswoman stopped by
My dad had set up his stall under the bridge
She wanted to buy three dozen coconuts
But only the big ones she said
My dad
The philosopher
Calmy said
Now looka here Sis
God
When He made man
He didn't make them all alike
No ma'am
He made some tall
Some short
Some fat
Some skinny
He didn't pick and choose which ones to create
So I guess if that plan could work for God
It oughta be able to work for you and me

I Used to Hear My Dad Say

We would be out at sea
In the little dinghy boat
Fishing
And I mean the fish would be biting
They would be really jumping as they say
And my dad
Who taught us everything he knew and could
Would say
Alright boys
Let's pack up
It's time to go
But Dad
No no my dad would reply
Determined and implacably resolute
Pack it up
It's time to go
We have to leave some for next time
Or for the other ones who are coming after us
That strange logic
What my dad would say

Would leave me and my brother scratching our heads
Not until many years later
And while studying as a student in the Pond
When I learned about the world's diminishing resources
And Jesus' disciples walking through the grain fields
Would I understand
The valuable lesson my dad was trying to teach

Milton

Life in the Puddle could have its drawbacks though
Cut off from the world like we were
In many ways it was a world unto itself
Lacking in knowledge and understanding
Sophistication
Or even compassion
For example
We had never heard of words like disabled
Arrested development
Mentally challenged
Or handicap
We were kids
And as far as we were concerned
You were either normal
Or crazy
This is where Milton came in
If I could see you now
Milton
Go back in time
Here is what I would say

Please forgive us
Milton
Forgive us for we knew not what we were doing
You used to sit by the roadside
The dusty sandy track that passed for road
In your burlap gown
Long and flowing like a slender girl's oversized and dirty dress
We didn't know any better
So we would shoo you away
When all you wanted to do was play
Even though you were a grey-haired old man
We didn't know Milton
Your arms were twisted and your fists all balled up
Your legs were like wobbly wooden crutches when you tried to run
Chase after us
Yes
You would try to run after us
How were we to know that you just wanted to play
No one had told us Milton
That you were just a child trapped in a man's body
Not even
Your grunting sounds
Your mouth twisted to the side
Everything about you
Milton
Was twisted and wobbly
We just saw you as a cripple
To be laughed at and taunted

Milton

Crippled funny and dumb

A laughingstock

Something to amuse ourselves with on the long walk home from school

We were just children

Milton

Foolish and ignorant

Trapped in a world of not knowing

Not caring

Not caring for anyone who could not walk talk or run like us

If I could see you now

Milton

Go back in time

Here is what I would say

Please forgive us Milton

Forgive us for we knew not what we were doing

When you would run

We would run too

Run away from you

Laughing

We would throw sticks and dry coconuts at you

And you would grunt and wobble after us

How could we

Senseless children as we were

Know that all you wanted to do was play

It was not until I left the Puddle did I fully understand

Feel the sting of shame and guilt

Truly understand what it means to be disabled

Mentally challenged
Or impaired
All I can say is ...
If I could see you now
Milton
Go back in time
Here is what I would say
Please forgive us Milton
Forgive us
Poor ignorant children in so many ways
Forgive us Milton
For we knew not what we were doing

Alton and the Dog

Like I said just now
Life in the Puddle was impoverished
In so many ways
Take for example how we looked at life
People were people
Animals
The ones you couldn't eat
Were all meant to be abused
Dogs and cats were strays
They never lived in anybody's house
Until
That is
The new government hired some teachers from England and the West Indies
This was long ago
And this was how we saw life
Most of the time
Through archaic lenses
Take for example Alton and the dog
The British teacher wanted us to go over to his house

He needed some help with moving some furniture
We were all excited
Skipping over the limestone rocks
That's when Alton spotted the dog
And in his excitement
Not knowing any better
Just wanting to be funny
And cruel
Alton kicked the dog
The dog yelped
We all laughed and scoffed
The British teacher was shocked
Horrified
He turned abruptly
Looked at us
Glared really
His brow all furrowed and his face turning even more pink
Yelled at us
Scolded us
Called us every name under the sun
Told us that we were incorrigible
And that we were
Mean
Cruel
And beyond vicious
Every last one of us
And that we were the wretched of the earth

I Love You, Matilda— Picky-Head and All

Matilda was the girl that everyone called picky-head
Because she always wore her hair in the natural
She never used any straightening comb
Or anything like that
Like the other girls
Matilda was dark-skinned
Satiny
Glowing and glistening in the Andros hot sun
We would see her down by the roadside
At the public well
She would be carrying two screechy empty buckets in one hand
In the other
She would be clutching two snotty-nose and unruly kids
Matilda's hair was always in an afro
Half plaited
And with a comb sticking out of it
The other girls who would pass by would laugh at Matilda

Call her picky-head
Just because she wore her hair that way
But with Matilda it was intentional
Deliberate
I found this out later
We
The boys
We loved Matilda
She was grown
And more mature than all of us
When we would say things out of the way to her
She would chase after us and pummel us with a soft fist
We loved Matilda
There was just something about her
Way back then
She didn't care about what other people thought or said about her
It was the way she carried herself
Her hair always in an afro
Half plaited
And with a comb always sticking out of it
When the other girls who passed by would say mean things to her
Matilda would just stare back at them
Looking piercingly right through them
As if they were glass
Matilda had a way about her
The way she swiveled and cocked her head
Cranked her neck

She could be bossy and sassy like that
My mom
Always overly protective of her baby boy
Took one look at Matilda and said
I don't want you having nothing to do with that girl
She is too fresh too fast and too forward
Except she would say frorward
Many years later after leaving the Puddle
And coming to the Pond
And seeing the likes of Pam Grier and Tamara Dobson on the big screen
Black women
Bold
Proud
Confident
Independent
And free
Sporting afros
Deliberately
Their hair all in the natural just like Matilda's
Except for the comb sticking out of them
Like Matilda they refused to let others define them
And like Matilda
They too were picky-heads you can say
Sporting their hair in the natural
Swiveling and cranking their necks
Cocking their heads to one side then the other just like Matilda
That air of freedom
That said I don't care world what you think

I am free
Free to be who I want to be
Free to be who I was born to be
It made me come to grips with my own perception of beauty
What was it
Was it a look
A certain attitude
Or did it radiate from within
Matilda
A proud Black girl
Growing up on the island of Andros
Bold
Proud
Confident
Independent
And free
Didn't care what anybody else saw
Or thought
Carrying herself gracefully
Just like Pam Grier and Tamara Dobson
Since then we have all grown
I know I have
And if I could see her now
Matilda
Here is what I would say with full-blown confidence
I love you Matilda
I love you
Picky-head and all

Love Never Dies

Who was it that said love is mortal
That love sometimes succumbs and dies
No
Love never dies
It just
Sadly
Unfurls its wings
Flapping them sadly
Dejectedly
And flies away
Hurt
To some nearby or faraway perch
Where it comes to rest
Gloomily
While it licks its wounds
Love does get tired though
Weary
Tired of all the fuss
Fights
The battles

When it does
It sadly bows out
Gives up
It has to
Or otherwise stand and fight
That it cannot do
To do so would betray self
Under the pressure of structures
Strictures
Of what we call society or conventions
So love
Under the strain
Sadness
Disappointments
Chooses to just pine away
Like Tristan and Isolde
Sick
Beaten
Badly bruised
And after many tussles wars and battles
And burdened down with much pain suffering heartache and hurts
Love
No
It doesn't die
Never
Love
No
Love never dies

It just resigns itself
Accepts moments of defeats
Sick
Beaten
Badly bruised
Love just unfurls its wings
Sadly
Disappointed again
And flies away
To some nearby or faraway perch
Where it rests gloomily to lick its wounds
And plots its triumphant return

After the Storm

When we were young and growing up in the Puddle
We knew how to really hunker down during the storm
Frightened and excited
Gleeful
But after the violence of the long days and nights
The rattling and the shaking
The constant slanted pounding of the shifting rain
The occasional slamming
The winds howling loudly stirring and churning madly
But always
Right after the long ordeal
We would venture out
Eager to see
Take in
The utter destruction
The crowning achievement of the always-brutal storm
We could hardly wait to see what all had been swept away
Was left
It was always a sight to behold
The strange calmness and beauty that blanketed the land

The dark lagoons of quiet peaceful waters that would be settled in the crossroads
And we would sail our coconut bark boats and yell at each other for cheating
All while splashing through the dark and murky waters
Our parents
Or some other grown ups
Would scold us
Tell us to get out of the water
The water
They would say
After the storm
Could make you sick
But we didn't mind
We just saw how all the dirt and the filth
That use to clutter our lives
Had all been washed away
Like a brand-new day
And everything just seemed so shiny and new
So peaceful
Clean
And calm
It always made us happy
Right after the storm

You Saved Me (An Ode)

You saved me
You saved my life
Hoisted me and carried me places I never dreamt
Gave me the strength
The legs and a foundation on which to stand
The power to outpace all my classmates
Impress my tutors
I was that sad and lonely little boy from Dickens
Until I found you
And you found me
Became my only friend
My trusted friend and companion
And as friends so often do
We poured ourselves into each other
Embraced often
And held each other close
Aloft
And kept each other safe
I was jealous
I would not loan you out or share you with another

Or let someone tear one of your delicate pages
Friends like you
Growing up in a world bereft of the likes of you
You became my treasure
My joy
I would chase after you
Wherever I could find you
Even though the others teased me
And called me a sissy
We laughed
And we cried
So many times
And over treacherous paths
And beautiful meadows we did go
Out of this world
And into worlds unimaginable
Yet you would tell me go ahead and imagine them
You instructed me
Took me to many places distant
You introduced me to friends you had inside of you
Knew
They became my friends too
Friends that lurked and floated between your pages
Like a beautiful game of hide and seek
Forever we will share
Cherish them
Oliver
Hamlet
Tom Sawyer

Snow White and the seven dwarfs
David when he slew Goliath
And Joseph and his coat of many colors
Peter and Jane
As they flew across the meadows
Oh
The things you have taught me
Sustaining
Lifting me higher
Enlightening
Like light that shone into darkened corners
Like a mother embracing a sad and lonely child
Nurturing
And teaching them
Preparing them
What a struggle it would have been if I didn't have you
To comfort me
Nurture me
Teach me and school me
My rock and foundation
Now I am flung into this cold and difficult world
This world of survival and competition
And all I have
Still
Are the tender thoughts of your loving embrace
The gift
And the gifts
You gave to me

My First Introduction to My Own Blackness

Growing up in the Puddle
A young kid
You didn't see color
Skin color
Nobody had time to discuss
Much less notice whether you were so-called black or white
We thought the whole world resembled and looked like us
I can still remember the first time I was introduced to my own skin color
My own blackness
I was about nine or ten years old
And a naval ship from the Pond had sidled noisily up to the rocks down by the Pit
Near our peaceful and quiet tiny settlement
And opened and slammed down its heavy metallic jaw
With a loud clankety clank
And a loud boom

Out streamed some men in green and brown clothing and wearing helmets
They looked like soldiers we had seen only in picture books
Some of them were light complected
Some dark brown like us
I remember the dark-complected ones were especially happy to see us
In a strange way we were happy to see them too
They must have known we were thirsty because they lowered and tilted their orange drinking jug
And gave us ice cold water
Perhaps they just wanted to be nice
Bond with us
We tilted our heads back and allowed the cool refreshing drink to first just trickle then cascade all over our faces
A little bit went into our mouths
The dark-complected ones were quite amused and happy to see us
Our unkempt raggedy and dirty shirts and pants
Our dirt-stained faces
As we huddled sheepishly together
They showed us how to slap
Smack hands
Down low
Then up high
And they would go
My man
Give me five
They never got tired of saying

My man

And

Give me five

It was infectious

And we started giving each other five on the sly

Then one of the light-complected ones

The leader we just assumed

Shouted

Hey Kunta Kinte

It's time to go

And

Let's get a move on

It must have been a joke

Because all of the light-complected ones laughed

They laughed uproariously

Then the dark-complected one

One of the ones that looked like us

Who had given us the ice-cold water to drink

Who had taken the time to slap hands with every last one of us

And say

My Brother

Give me five

And

Alriggghttt

Right on

And made us in some strange way feel a sense of pride

He turned to go

To join the others

But before he went

He had a word for the light-complected one
He said
Hey Jack
What you bothering me for man
Can't you see I am with my people
And he turned
Took one last endearing look at us
Huddled and slightly jostling like a knot of dark penguins
Still fascinated and slightly amused by us
He winked
Raised his arm
Clenched his fist
And said
Okay all you fine young Black Brothers
You be cool you hear

I Ain't No African

In this life
Life can be so sweetly confusing
And amusing
Like this time I am talking to an old friend
We had known each other for quite some time
Had gone to school together
Then I had left home
Thrust into the wide world that is the reality of the Pond
This new compelling reality can force you to question who and what you are
Cause new realizations and consciousness to arise
And set in
She was young
Beautiful
Black and satin
Looked every bit like the young women I had met at the university
Young Black women
Black and satin
Africans

From places like Niger
Nigeria
And Ghana
We were having fun
Though we were both half serious
She was standing in the doorway striking a pose
I was ribbing her
Telling her how she looked every bit like girls I had met from
Niger Nigeria and Ghana
That's when she said it
Playfully but half serious
Lunging with her voice
Don't call me that she said
Call you what
Call me no African
I ain't no African
Then she charged
I know how you people go she said
Half laughing
Half serious
As soon as you'll go off
Go away to wherever
You'll does come back all confused
With all sorts of crazy ideas
You might be from there
Not me
She said she was from the Puddle
Through and through
Born and raised

And she was not from no Africa
Dark
Dark and satin
Dark like Niger Nigeria and Ghana
The West Coast
Dark like a Yoruba or Asanti princess
She said
I didn't come from no Africa
I don't know nothin' bout no Africa
Now she was pretending
Pretending to not know what I meant
Pretending to be angry
Vex
I ain't never been to no Africa she laughed
Sheepishly and confused
And I ain't fixin' to go no time soon
You and your confused friends like Marcus Garvey can go there if you want
To where was it again she laughed
Nigeria or Liberia
Or was it Sierra Leone
That's it
Sierra Leone
She hesitated
Not sure
One of those places she said vacantly
But not me
Like I said
I already told you

I ain't no African
And
Thinking she could shut the case
Slam it shut
Seal her argument
She said
And furthermore
And according to my family tree
Her hand pressed across her chest for greater emphasis
My family history
Which I have checked
I clearly couldn't have come from no Africa
Hardly able to maintain a straight face now
She said that according to her family history
And her family tree
She insisted
She was half Danish
Part Irish
And some part Cherokee

Speaking of Africa

I sat there
Perched on my little old rickety chair
By the roadside
Against the chain-linked fence
Trying to write this poem
My pen wavering
Tapping
Nervously
Unproductively
Upon my compressed lips
I watched
Squinting
Quizzically
Slightly amused
Because the sight looked vaguely familiar
Reminiscent of a time long gone
In a different place
So long
It seemed another life
As from another life and time

My mom
Her hands in her Kimbo
Her cutlass
Her only tool that day
Dangling by her side
She had taken a well-deserved break
From tending the stubborn weeds in the front yard
A neat little pile of sweet potatoes sat nearby
To meet my aunt
Auntie Manda
Over by the fence
It was as if they had seen each other in the distance
From afar
My Auntie Manda
The one who lived right across the street
My Auntie Manda
The one who was so creative
Resourceful
Made the best cassava and potato bread you ever tasted
Cared for us like we were her own kids
Whenever my mom was away
Gone to Nassau
Auntie Manda was the one who would always send over a hot cooked meal
Morning noon and afternoons
Now
Now their souls were having a meeting
There they stood
Not seeing or touching the fence between them

Like two sisters
Soul sisters
My mom with her hand in her Kimbo
My Auntie Manda
Arms folded
Gracefully
Dexterously
Balancing a bundle of sugarcane on her head
They chatted
They talked and they laughed
Whiling the time away
It was a sacred time and it didn't matter
At this precious moment
In this moment
Neither one had anything better they would rather do
Or was as important
They chatted
Laughed
And chatted some more
I looked at them from the perch of my little old rickety chair
By the roadside
Leaning against the chain-linked fence
Trying to write this poem
My mom
Her hand in her Kimbo
The dirt-stained cutlass still in her hand
Dangling by her side
My Auntie Manda
Dexterously

Effortlessly
Doing this balancing act with her bundle of sugarcane on her head
The scene itself was so far removed
Yet reminiscent
Perfectly so
Reminiscent of a time long gone
So long ago
That it seemed like another life
A portrait of far-flung
And long-gone times
In a distant place
That vacant distant sort of look in their eyes
As they just stood
Chatted
Laughed
Would pause for what seemed like hours
Not a word being spoken
Just that certified
And understandable bond that existed between them
Like two sisters
Soulmates
That bond that spoke loud and clear
Without uttering a sound
Of the joys and the pain
That sisterhood of the pain
Suffering
Tinged with joy and love built up over the years
And I whispered to myself

Yes
That's Africa
And my pen came to life also
And whispered right back at me
Yes
That's Africa
That's Africa alright

My Mom and All Her Sisters

The things you think about when you are in the Pond
And still dreaming of the Puddle
My mom and her four sisters for instance
My mom was one of five sisters
They all were like carbon copies of each other
Strong
Determined
Independent
And rowdy
They could do anything a man could
As a matter of fact
When my mom got tired of asking my dad to do something
She would just suck her teeth in disgust
And go do it herself
The men
Most of them
When I was growing up
Smoked pipes
Especially the men from the Baptist Church up on top of the hill

They would store their half-smoked pipes on the roof of the clapboard structure we called a tent
The tent
Or stall
Was where mostly the women sold tarts fried chicken and bottled sodas at special church events
During the service the men
Most of them deacons and ushers in the church
Would take pipe-smoking breaks
Now my mom and her four sisters weren't going for that look
A pipe dangling out of their mouths like a man
They were too proper and dignified for that
So they would take the tobacco
A big wad of tobacco
Stuff it in a pot
Add a little baking soda
Don't ask me why
Add plenty of water
And let it all boil on the open fire for hours
Then they would let it cool
Store it in jars
And as they worked in the yard
Or before going to bed
They would help themselves to a swig
A mouthful of this thick concentrated le jus
The idea was to hold it
Hold it
And just hold it
In your mouth

They would hold it for hours like that sometimes
And from time to time
Spitting it out just like a man
Whenever I couldn't go to sleep
Or I was just feeling miserable and out of sorts as a kid
My mom would give me some
Just hold it in your mouth she would say
Don't swallow it
It will calm you down
Calm your nerves
Help you go to sleep
I don't know about the calming my nerves part
But it sure would send the whole room whirling twirling spinning and tumbling
Then she would say now spit it out
Only I had already swallowed it by mistake
Now go back to bed
And I could remember walking back to our room
The room I shared with my brother
What an experience
Walking
Real tipsy
Like a little drunken sailor on the rough high seas
It was always a feat
Making it
All the way back to my bed
Just in time to fall soundly asleep
Sleeping all the way through the night
Like a little babe in a manger

Like Shifting Sand

Nothing is stable in the Pond
Life changes every day
People flit in and out of your life
You hardly remember their names
And you forget all about them a few months later
And life just goes on
One moment they are there
The next moment you look up and they are gone
Like how this big truck pulled up the other day
It was parked in front of my neighbor's house
I went out to see what all the fuss and commotion were about
My neighbor hopped down off the truck to greet me
Peeled off his dirty pair of gloves
Oh yes
I meant to come over to tell yuh he said
It's been fun knowing you guys for the last couple of months
But we are moving up north back to Chicago
And just like that they were gone
Out of our lives
Not so in the Puddle

Where you can know the same people all your life
The same houses
The same people moving around in those houses
Everyone is an Uncle or Auntie or Cousin So and So
And everybody greets you
Loves on you
And cares deep down for you
My dad and my uncle for example
They were brothers
They built their houses right next to each other across the road
Auntie Manda
Amanda
Except we call her Auntie Manda
Half not knowing any better
Half lovingly
Auntie Manda
The talented creative and industrious woman as much a mom to us as our own
She was known for her sweet potato and cassava bread
Nobody could bake sweet potato and cassava bread quite like Auntie Manda
Just like my mom was known for her light and fluffy baked white bread
Her bennie cakes
Her coconut cakes and tarts
We traded meals
If my mom was gone
We would get a meal coming across the street twice
Sometimes three times a day
The same would be true if Auntie Manda was gone

It was love
And they knew how busy our dads were
Just tradition
Here in the Pond however
No one cares
Life changes every day
People move in
They move out of each other's lives
It's like shifting sand
You see neighborhoods today
The next day they are torn down
And they become parking lots
Another strip mall
Where did those people go
The ones you knew just for a little while
Once in a while you wonder
Then you don't care
Life in the Pond is always moving
Fleeting
Transient
Moving away
Moving on
Not necessarily to a better place
Just to a different place
Sometimes out of necessity
Circumstances
It's circumstances they all say
Just constantly moving
Just like shifting sand

Conflicted and Torn

So many people I know
Live conflicted lives
Torn between two worlds
The world they left
And the one they find themselves stuck in
Hopelessly torn
In so many cases
Between stagnation
Limited expectations
Limited accomplishments
Too few to hang their hats on
Or to allow them to return to the places they call home
Where there are limited opportunities to stretch and to dream
Grow
Provide a life for oneself and one's family
Or it is too violent
And/or corrupted
In this land that always seems to hold out so much promise
Hope
Peace

Prosperity
At least you can breathe
Dream
Reach
You see life in the Pond is different from the puddles we come from
Here
It is not so much who you know as what you know
It is here too
Just not so much
With few opportunities back in the Puddle
You just feel it more
It is more palpable
You feel compelled to just get up and leave

They All Look at Me and Wonder

They all look at me and wonder
That's how life is in the Pond
They look at me and wonder out loud
Right to my face
Ah your islands they say
So beautiful
Like paradise
What made you want to leave
And I look at them
And I just smile
Sometimes
Life is just too complicated to explain

In the Pond

In the pond is where I was born
Reborn
Where I found Him
Where He found me
Where He gave me birth
A second birth
Where I spent most of my days
Where my life was altered
Rearranged
Changed
Fundamentally
Changed for the better
Changed forevermore
It was in the Pond
After I was born
Reborn
After He had given me birth
Born anew
Where my life began to take shape
Where my eyes were opened

And the power of God
Began to clarify things to me
Why He hoisted me
Lifted me
Brought me to this place
My own Egypt
Far from the land of my birth
God was with me
This I do know
All through my journeys
All through the battles
I am a fruit
Not the only
But one of many
Blessed
Brought to life
Maturity
Fullness
Ripeness
In order to reach back and help feed the others
Those we had to leave behind

Thank God for Ronald Reagan

My wife and I
Talking
We are sitting in front of the TV
Reminiscing
Remembering
Exactly how long we have been in this country
On TV
They are showing pictures of the crisis at the border
The controversy
The consternation in this country right now
So many of their faces set like flint against immigrants
We are blessed
And we both know it
My wife
She wants to thank God we at least made it
Thank God she says for amnesty
Then I remind her that it was in the time of Ronald Reagan
No she blurts

A Republican president
Yes I said
Well
She said
Thank God for life
For us
The good ole US-of-A
And thank God for Ronald Reagan

We Used to Take It All for Granted

We
For I was one of them
Who missed it
Couldn't even see it
Realize it
The beauty of it
We would just take it all for granted
Growing up in the Puddle
Strolling along white sandy beaches
Diving in the blue hole
Tossing our lines out into the sea from the shore
Catching shads
Narrow shads
Hangees
See them jumping and prancing right clear out of the crystal blue glassy water
Breaking and shattering it
Bonefish

Old wives
Always something to catch
Something to eat
Sitting on a sand dune
Basking in the glow and the balmy breeze
Peaceful
Open to the world
The sweet gentle breeze blowing
Sucking on sugarcane
But never quite appreciating
The world you are in
Been blessed with
A part of God's wonderful creation
I look back now
And oh how I wish
Things were different
That my eyes would have been open way back then
That I could see
And appreciate
That little slice of life
Of heaven
That which was mine
My own little slice of heaven
Splashes and gentle strokes
Streaked not splattered
Like brilliant paint brushed onto a canvas
And stretched out
As if it were on an easel
Such magnificent hues

Blue
Dark blue and light
Where sky meets water
Green blue and crystal clear
The sea
The sunlight bouncing and shimmering off it
Right there and in front of me

About the Author

Bertram Smith is an author, educator, speaker, and poet who shares his love for the culture, beauty, and history of his birthplace, The Bahamas. He is the author of the poetry collection *From the Puddle to the Pond* (2020), the middle-grade adventure fiction novella *The Blue Hole* (2021), and the Christian living nonfiction book *Through the Battles without the Scars* (2024). He is currently working on several other books to encourage others who are walking through difficult times in their lives.

With an extensive background teaching in public school, colleges, and university settings and active in church ministries over many years, Bertram also enjoys reading, writing, cooking, fishing, and spending time with his family. He is the proud father of two beautiful daughters, Falashade and Jamani. Bertram lives with his beautiful, darling wife, Leslie, in Atlanta, Georgia.

You can connect with Bertram on Facebook on the page "Books to Inspire Us."

About the Illustrator

Leroy Patrick Estime-Sweeting was born and raised in the Bahamas. Lee has one younger brother, an up-and-coming attorney at law. Lee is a well inspired artist by heart. He believes that "creativity and color is a string connected to the heart." Lee is also currently working as a server at an astonishing restaurant. Lee loves working with people, doing his best to make them happy. Lee also looks forward to becoming a highly successful architect in the future. Finally, Lee is also the CEO of Santos Portraits & Art & Santos Freelancers Co-operation.

"It has also been my pleasure to work with the author of this book, Mr. Bertram Smith. Great guy! And as time goes on, I have no doubt, our relationship in the realm of writing and art will grow enormously."

www.ingramcontent.com/pod-product-compliance
Lightning Source LLC
LaVergne TN
LVHW010326070526
838199LV00065B/5671